AN OPTIMISTIC VISION

PANCHATAPA BHATTACHARJEE

Table of Content

Table of Content

A Merry Child

1. An aspiration

Growing in the Greeneries,

Aspired to charm like a butterfly!!

Running through the soothing scenarios,

She wanted to glow like a Firefly!!

Gazing through the Sky,

She used to feel a humorous Shy!!

Chasing beautiful memories Behind the Stars,

Her ambition was to go beyond the Society Bars!!

A glimpse to her Daily Routine,

Imposes a Charge on her Discipline!!

She has always been an Early Riser,

The Journals and Books made her Wiser!!

All the day, she used to be a multi tasked,

She was an inspiration to many as a brisker!!

As days passed, her family started going through critical crisis,

At an early age of Nineteen, she held her family tight, to not to make them fall into Abyss!!

With her wit, she passed the Exams for a School Teacher,

With her patience, she started coaching Students after the School Hours, and became a Preacher!!

She had become one of the most sourced Bread Earner for her family,

She eventually started to hold onto the responsibilities steadily!!

A strong mindset and a smart look helped her in communicating for various Social Tasks,

Apart from all the regular chores, she had become an Active Member in Women's Rights!!

2. The Marriage

Fulfilling all the responsibilities at Home and for the Society,

She was the only left unmarried, amongst her Friends!!!!

Though she was happy and enjoying her Blends!!!

But at her home, it became a major cause of Anxiety.

"They are coming to see you for Marriage" suddenly a call went to her at her School,

Though she was reluctant and hesitant but she had to act like a Cool!!

With all her Wit and Beauty, the proposal was fixed happily,

And with this, she started nourishing her marriage Lovingly.

Adjustments and Trust were her Strongest Boons,

Sharing all about Life, days passed to Moon through Noon!!!!

After a span of two Years, they had to leave the house and family and build their own home,

For the purpose of work transfer and commitment, they started housing their Peaceful Dome.

Caring for each other, mending the needs of each other,

They started living Life through Thicks and Thins!!!!

Grazing through Hopes and Laughter, where Grief never used to bother,

Merrily they were through to Life with a Light Within!!!!

3. The Death Bed

"Tring Tring" The phone rang, "Your husband is no more"!!

She exploded in a bust of Tears Of Shock!!

All the Happiness and Moments were sudden Locked,

And the Sorrow scattered from Zenith to Core!!!!!

Sudden Calm of gesture is all around,

Bewildering nature stands to be ground!!!!

Collection of memories scattered all over the floor!!

A never healing Pain had summoned her Door!!!!

Gone are those days of Contentment,

Hailing Storms and Destruction everywhere!!!!

Gone are those days of Peacefulness,

Sorrow and Grievance Everywhere!!!!

A strong Hurricane had split her soul and mind,

A soothing space she was unable to find!!!!

Though she never complaint, she never denied the situation!!

She startled but continued the journey towards her life's mission!!!!

4. A Rising Hope

Amidst all the chaos and abrupt circumstance,

A little ray of sunshine barged into her life!!

Her emerged desire for a fruitful Life came into Alive!!

And ,she had given birth to a Beautiful Baby Girl ,One Year Hence!!!!

With the baby Girls' existence, she and her surroundings changed,

With her little footsteps, the Baby girl kindled her joyfulness around!!

With her cute wiggles, she made the home into a beautiful cascade!!!

And the days passed by!!!!

The baby girl was very much talented and oriented towards her goal,

Whatever she does, she used to achieve success!!

To each and everything she does, She used to do with her pure heart and soul!

Gradually she became the only Inspiration of the Coalesce!!!

5. The Ambitious Lassie

Days into weeks and weeks into months, months into year and years into decades!!

As in, many years were passed with this continuity,

And The Baby girl is now a grown up Lady!!

She had grown into a Joyful Witty!!

From Schools to Colleges, she used to spread her Aura!!

Wherever she goes, whatever she does, she used to bloom like a Colorful Flora!!

Like mother like Daughter, she was confident, cheerful and Smart!!

She was versatile enough to Dance, Theatre and Art!!

Every morning she used to wake up at Four, yoga and meditation were her first priority,

Once after completion of Yoga, she used to bathe and take part in spiritual activity!

A non disturbance of two hours of Study, accomplished her morning Duty,

A delicious breakfast prepared at home by her mother was her Morning Grabby!!

An Ocean of Targets for the life, she had wished for,

A sea of Insightful Desires, she had wished for,

With dedication, optimism and honesty, she had achieved all!!

And Finally she was a representative of her Country, and became an Administrative Officer!!!!

6. A Happy Ending

She has become the Pride of her Mother,

That Happy soul, had finally began to live and Laughter!!

All the sacrifices had resulted into a successful story!!

And the darkness converted into a Night's Glory!!

Again those Greeneries were protruding a mesmerizing Elegance,

And the Scenarios everywhere turned into Magnificence!!

Everywhere there is a Humble Peace of Fauna,

All the chaos around her, turned into a Comfort Sauna!!

All throughout these Painful Years,

All throughout these Deceitful Years,

Her mother never followed the path of dishonesty and pessimism!!

Through her motivation and strength, she had nurtured her baby, with her optimism!!!!

She had cried, she felt helpless, but she never broke her soul!!

She was heartbroken, she was homeless, but she never allowed herself and the Baby to deviate from their Goal!!

With purity of soul, mind and heart!!

She won the battle of Life and her core screamed forever to the Contentment Blart!!

Moral :

Wherever there is a Positive Mindset and Honesty, Whatever the Situation is, Success And Happiness Chases!!

An Ordinary Girl

She lives in the city with a full of roars,

Often she ponders whether she can reach to the peace of shores!!!!

Diving onto the sea of love, she moves ahead courageously,

And as usual, the world seems to behave befriendly!!!

As the time passes, her strength starts fading,

And She walks through the Timber of positivity with a great wading!!!

Beneath the solidarity, she trembles with her identity,

She understands now, with this era of stardom,

And showcase, Only, quantity succeeds quality!!!!!

With these chaos of ambiguity all around,

She decides to go on and on until she finds her destiny!!!!!

With all the positive intentions,

She decides to lure the magical intuitions!!!!

A glory in hand , and a beauty in order,

A Fiery Bond that lasts longer!!

An elegant hour and a splendid period,

That she believes would be her sooner!!

A Delightful Cake

7. The Pathway

"Son, come to the house, fast, lunch time it is", a voice surfaced onto the atmosphere,

Although he was reluctant, still he adhered!!

His Father was waiting for him to start eating,

His mother was eagerly serving the delicious food for feeding!!

"Maa, the Food is really Tasty " he smiled and greeted his mother,

He had some of them and requested his mother to pack some , rather!!

Father asked him " Son, for whom do you want to pack this Food?"

He replied, "I want to feed the poor working at our field to Enjoy Some!"

Father smiled and lovingly patted his Son's Back,

He went to the field to distribute the food in the Shadow Shack!!

Once after he went, his father murmured to his mother " We are lucky to have a son like this "

Hopefully he never changes ,and behold this Kindness towards other, forever like this!!!

While he was returning from the crop Fields in the late evening,

He saw a vendor selling some food item "At 5, get 6, At 5, Get 6 ", screaming!!

There was a huge crowd gathering, gradually,

Out of his curiosity, he started strolling towards the shop slowly!!

8. The Discovery

He goes to the vendor, and found a small piece of cake with a red cream over it, wrapped in a silver Foil,

He asks the Vendor, " Hello Uncle, can you please tell me what is so special in this cake, which is urging people to buy over and over again?"

Vendor replied, " Son, I have added a secret ingredient which is not available in the market and can only be felt only when you eat this cake once!!"

He surprisingly says " Can you name the Ingredient, Please?"!!

Vendor says, " Sorry Son, as I told earlier , it's a secret and if I tell, I will not be able to justify my Toil!!"

He says, " Ok, Uncle, please give me 6 cakes, I will have and take them for my family, "

And he leaves from the place and starts walking toward his house!!

While he was walking down the road, a little poor girl came to him and said " Brother,do you have some food?, can you please give me a little portion?"

And, he immediately gave 2 pieces of cake to her, and said " Be Happy Always!! "

He went on and on towards his home,

Till he sees a white Dorm,

Eager was his curiosity, and he was zealous,

And the next minute, he was inside the Dorm!!

"Wow, what a Beauty ", he started gasping,

With wonders around, his eyes started raffling!!

He was mesmerized with the vintage elegance,

His mind was proof reading the unique eloquence!!!!

9. The Determination

A sudden sense of upliftment touched his conscience,

A diligence to strive the hard, stuck to his voice within!!

Although the roads were ambiguous, But he was
determined,

To achieve what he had decided ,pondering about the
Scene, in the dorm!!

And He felt the sense of right within!!

The next day when he was having lunch with his family,
he murmured " I want to study further and become a
Teacher to nurture knowledge all over the society, "

I want to raise the underprivileged children, with
education, so that they can bring sobriety!! "

" Son, what are you saying? ", his father replied " The time
has already eloped, you are a full grown Adult now with
no scope of education!! How will you start all over?"

He replied, " Father, I want to rectify my mistake which I
had done to the society by not educating myself and now I
want to be a prover!! "

He was adamant, and he was composed,

He was dealing the situation, with his confidence utmost

His father says " Okay, Son, I am with you, please go ahead, but please remember that you have to pass through several strenuous situations in order to achieve, "

Please donot loose hope, and let the pessimism archive!! "

Once again, he started his education, with complete dedication,

Nonetheless, One by one, he walked towards his mission!!

Though he did not know what will be his destination,

A lure of freedom for the poorest was his temptation!!

10. Hard Work Pays Off

With continuous struggles and juggles,

And With his tremendous efforts,

The day has come when the result is to be declared soon,

With his hope and positivity, his accomplishments shall rise high to Moon!!

And here comes the moment of nervousness and fear,

"I cannot accept the consequence of failing, for the society " he drear!!

" No matter what, I will not loose hope " he murmurs to himself,

"I will have my other plans to cope "he says to himself.

With flying hues, he was one of the Top performing Candidate,

This strong achievement of his, was only a Bait!!

It was a bait for the privileged to help sponsoring the education for the poorest,

It was a bait for the society to accept the dearest!!

A long run to go, a bigger road to walk,

He may be alone and frightened ,but he is surrounded by inspiring thoughts!!

Which never had made him coward!!

He is now stepping into his real journey of completing his mission with the special ingredient ,that, the delightful cake's vendor told him one day!!

And Which is Love!!

11. The Secret Ingredient

A while ago, when he was returning back to home ,from his institution,

He came across a strange situation!!

A little child was crying and searching for his mother to feed him,

While he could not find her, he started walking down the road!!

While that little child was immature to understand the matter of safety on the road,

May be an unseen circumstance can make the little child blowed

Out of his concern, he holds those little fingers of the child and consoled him,

" Your mother will be at home soon, lets walk towards your home " he bestowed him!!

While walking towards the home, he bought a chocolate to the little child to make him smile,

Instead, the child refused to eat and continued to be in pain, tears were all around his cheeks like a chyle!!

He continued to engage the child with small conversations of animals and birds,

Though the little child stopped crying , but his eyes were charred!!

A moment later, his mother came running and took him to her lap,

A plate of white rice, salt and water took him to nap!!

He was surprised and shockingly asked, " How did a simple plate of water and rice, made him so comfort while the chocolate which was full of sweets and happy hormones could not make him stop shedding his Tears?"

To this , the Mother smiled and said, " Dear , the plain rice and water had the special ingredient that is My Love, which the chocolate could not afford even if it costs you high and wrapped into sheers!!"

And in the next moment he immediately realizes, what the Cake Vendor had said him once,

The special ingredient which he adds onto his cake is His Love Punce!!

He understood that wherever he goes and whatever he wants,

If he can add Love to it, he can absolutely gain the Success Dunt!!!!

12. The Victory

In the dorm, where he had walked on, and wandered onto its beauty!!

He witnessed a gathering of children, learning and helping each other in gaining knowledge on their own,

Where he witnessed the struggle which they were doing ,

While working on the fields at daytime and continuing studies at night,!!

They used to take the responsibilities of their families as little grown!!

That day, he had seen the eagerness of these poor children to grow high,

That day, he had seen the persistence of these children to succeed and exemplify!!

He took an Oath to educate for rebuilding the society,

Where people can build well to do homes for their family ,with no impropriety!!

And from the first day of his success, he started practicing Free Teaching to all the underprivileged children,

He had convinced their poor parents to send their children for Free Education,

Gradually, the circumstances begin to change,

And a whole lot of knowledge was all around the corner,

Those poor children had hold their mind strong to uphold their village to adorner!!

Eventually, the condition of the village began to improve,

With the achievements of the children, prosperity began to groove!!

Everyone understood the importance of education and knowledge,

Without accepting, they would have remained in a state of Haulage!!

He fought a tough battle, which was a cold grapple!!

He tout a positive change in the living of all,

It was an ambition which was high and tall!

Nevertheless, he continued to chase, to make his village, a Learning Chappell!!

Moral :

Love, Dedication and Courage are the secret sauces to any Achievement. There is no age to initiate any Improvement Plan on ourselves.

A Hermit

Once upon a time,

There was a happy hermit,

And where he goes and what he does,

How tough the path is, but he never quits!!

One Day, while he was farming,

He saw something very enchanting!!

And he wants to engulf the magic,

Thus he steps towards the magmic!!

""Ohhhhhh",The Hermit screams" That rosy flower which
is blooming as gold,

And that can be never sold,

Up the sky and down the earth,

Belittle thy worth!!

I do take the venge of it's blossom,

That makes my life a Gotham!!"

And the hermit returns to his doom ,

He nourishes the rosy flower that often blooms!!

Thus, he now is never alone,

The aura of that rosy flower is his backbone!!

He do take the courage there after,

And the hermit lives happily ever after!!

The Good Intention

13. A Hustle

Once, there was a very loyal soldier,

Who used to be his master's wonderful Protector!!

Half of his day ends with his master's caricature,

And he used to spend the rest of the time in Surrounding Nature!!

One day when he was passing by the Forest,

He heard a Screaming Sound running into the Woods with utmost sorest!!

He, being a saviour, could not resist himself in finding the helpless sound,

He being the courageous, could not stop himself from being bound!!

He started following the sound, and reached until the bank of a River,

As he was looking around, suddenly he heard a voice, " Who are You?"

He said in response, " I am a Protector, Leave the Person you had captivated, Don't Linger!! "

" I have not captivated any person with me, Go Away from here!!"

He responded, " In my country everyone is safe and healthy, if someone tries to harm anyone!!

I do not hesitate to bring out my weapon "

As he turned back, a well to do man along with a Woman who has quite scars, comes out from the deep,

And the man responds, " Whoever you are, don't try to interfere in between me and my Wife and vanish soon!"

He responded," Don't befool me, by telling she is your wife, and even if she is your wife, you do not have any rights to torture her!!"

And suddenly the Lady responded, " No No Sir, he is my well wisher, my husband, please leave him, you can go from here "

After listening to the Woman, he got into the confusion of helping her!!

"Why will my husband torture me Sir, please understand and Leave "once again the Lady affirmed

And the Soldier left, although he felt something mischievous!!

14. The Penalty

As the days were passed, the soldier often used to hear the same screaming voice,

And every time, he did not have any courage to help,

Sometimes, the voice used to get converted to noise,

The passers would not have bothered, and the Woman used to Yelp!!

One day, as the soldier was passing by the same pavement

He witnessed two children with deep cuts and soars,

At the same moment, he also witnessed the Woman wiping the blood effacement!!

This time, he could not resist and stood near the Women, but she ignored!!

"Please let me know, what has happened here? " The soldier Asked

" I know, I should not have interfered any, but after looking these children soars and cuts, I could not resist myself ", the soldier murmured!!

The Woman replied, " Please go away from here , I request you to not to amplify my difficulties further!!

And please do not tell this to anyone, what you have seen here!!!!"

The soldier felt bad and was helpless,

The Woman was adamant to not to involve him onto this weird Situation!!

The Soldier replied, " I respect your decision ,and I will not ask you regarding this anymore!!

I will not let anyone know about this state, but I would like to request you to bring yourself out of this situation "

To take care of yourself and children, As they are priceless!!!!

15. The Promise

Does it matter the way, the soldier approached the Woman?

Or does it matter how bad the circumstance is!!

Although the Woman was struggling, but she was confident enough to handle,

Hence, she survived for herself and children by Happiness Ampoule!!

From the next day onwards, the people passing by never heard any such voice around

No Screaming noise all around!!

Everything was at peace, And the Woman can nowhere be seen!!

As promised, the soldier had never disclosed the scene!!

A year passed by now, and the master fell ill and was bedridden!!

The master believed that now its time to let go of his responsibilities and crown someone who deserves!!

He always used to believe that his soldier is the most authentic and a gem hidden!!

And he decided to make his soldier the Magnificent Master under whom the rich heritage will be preserved

Few Years Hence, the Master died and the Soldier was in the thrown serving his people with utmost Safety and Care

With a wrench of Protection, he wanted to uplift the living of his people by Urbanisation that can Flare!!

He had always a Good Intention towards everyone,

And His Dedicated Works towards the people could be a Prover to Anyone!!

16. The Proposal

To refine his country and his populace by urban sprawl,

He began to invite senior officials from the Globe overall!!

Few would have suggested to convert the rich heritage of the country into Modernisation,

Where some suggested to demolish the old Culture to Urban Rejuvenation!!!!!

He wanted to urbanise his populace but not with the cost of demolishing the Rich Heritage,

He wished to flaunt the Heritage to the World, it was his Envisage!!

Though this seemed to be a Far away Dream,

Nevertheless, he did not loose his vision and walked again for this Futuristic Beam!!

And a miracle happened the next day,

A young Boy stepped with this amazing Idea of Outplay

And the boy spoke," Your Majesty , why cannot we move our country from Monarchy to Democracy?"

He replied, " Young Boy , can you please elaborate more on this?"

" Your Majesty, Democracy will help you to protect the Rich heritage of the Country by allowing you the rights to Speak and Preserve"

"Democracy shall help you to bring Urbanisation to the country by giving populace the rights to Education,

This will eventually provide them the Rights to Vote, to choose their own Saviour , the one whom they think can better serve"

Democracy will eventually bring out the best in People, and make them Responsible"

17. The Confrontation

"Wow, this Young Boy has exactly voiced out the thought, which I was looking ",he murmured to himself

"Thank you Young Boy, for this precious suggestion", He replied

"Your Majesty, This is my Honour, to do something for my populace and country!!

"Let us work together and make the welfare of this country as our Prime Priority"

The young boy was working with his complete dedication

He was diligent enough with his honest Intention!!

Grooming the mass and gaining their Confidence and Trust!!

True was his determination and Entrust!!

"I can resemble the Young Boy to someone with the same mindset of never loosing!!

I can resemble the Young Boy to the Woman I met, with this same strength of moving!!"

"Young Boy, Where are you from and how did you land up here ?", he asked the Boy while he was working One Day!!

"I belong to this Country!! Due to some unforgettable moments, I had to leave this country to protect my family from Slay"

He understood that this is the same Boy whom he had seen with Deep Cuts and Soars!!

He understood that he is the Son of that Woman who had to flee away!!

"Ok Young Boy, please don't worry and please feel safe enough to bring back your family!!"

"Sure, Your Majesty, Thank You for the Assurance ", The Young Boy Replied!!

18. Face Off

After listening to the Young Boy, He was lost and Curious!

Though as promised, he would not interfere in the Woman's story,

Still his sympathy towards the Woman was not Spurious!!

All these Years, he just desired to see that Woman's Glory!

He announced an arrangement for a Feast for achieving victory in establishing democracy,

And where, of course, he invited the families of entire contour!!

He was aware that the Woman never want to discuss her sorrow with anyone,

Still he insisted to meet her to congratulate her on her Freedom and Cure!!

The Event Day had begun with grand Music and Celebration,

Within a span of few seconds, and the whole Country was turned into a Luminous Nation!!

"I hope you are fine and Healthy " a resembling voice had crawled down his Ears,

He turned back and the Woman burst down into Tears!!

" I was rude , I was hard enough to behave inhuman with you "

In that situation, I had become a complete nuisance!!

But, I had carefully marked your words and now for my Children, I had to live a life well to do!!

I made myself so strong and worked hard just to ensure a prosperous life for my children, as someone said, They are priceless!!"

He smiled and replied,"I always wanted to see your Glory,

I knew that one day you will achieve the Victory!!

I was eagerly waiting to see you and your children smile,

And strolling with the Pride, down the Aisle!!"

moral:

Its okay to let go of the situation we cannot interfere. Its okay not let people dive into their perceptions and thoughts upon you. If you have a good intention, eventually the people will come to know one day.

A Solitary Soul

Someday somehow under the sky,

I found a little soul, full of shy

Little does he speak, Feeble does he walk

He was timid, though he used to Squawk.

The Little Soul was full of Melody,

More he sings, more the Praises Surrounds Merrily!!

A Good Lovely Afternoon, while he was resting beneath
the Blue,

While a hermit was passing, and his Lullaby turns into
Parody!!!!

The Little Soul was kind and Sober, though the Hermit
was rude and brutal!!

While the Hermit was trying to rob him ,the little soul raised his voice and said, "I donot have anything to give you,Sir!! Please forgive me!!"

The Hermit said,"Boy ,why do you say so? When you have your magical voice, a kind heart and a beautiful soul inside you !!You have to lend all these things to me!!"

The Little soul said, "If you can compliment my voice, if you can understand the soul I am ,then you must also be a wonderful person!!Why are you walking down the path of glee??"

The Hermit Replied, " I was a wonderful person indeed by Heart, but the society rejected me for being kind , naïve and beautiful , Hence I chose this path of decree!!"

A Dilemma Inside

As he closes his eyes,

The Roar of Confusion Sighs.

Upon trying to find Insights,

He looses his way Inside.

A Sudden wave of Pain overwhelms his mind,

To let go of his Trust and not to be Kind.

A surprising Moment of Shock Shatters His Belief

To let go of his Sympathy and Not to Be in Grief

A feeling of insecurity fogs his intelligence,

A gloomy cloud of Anger fogs covers his sightedness!!

The one with the most distinctive future sight,

Now has become the most difficult plight!!

Often he feels to be threatened by his own Guilt of
Insobriety,

Often he feels to be the culprit for his own Empathy!!

Although he tries to remove this ambiguity and find a
path to Foster,

Gradually he starts training his mind , where the Sun rises
in the Oster!!

A continuous war between his mind and Soul frightens
him up,

Often he feel , the need of Finding his Escape Cup,

"Keep Moving " The Core Within he , dreams!

" I shall stand up, Even If I Fail " His Confidence
Continues to Scream.

A Foster Home

19. Act of Kind

A Gloomy Day , and Clouds are High,

A Rainy Day, and Noons are Shy!!

A little Girl was coming back from school, covering her head with an Umbrella,

Playing in the water, stuck in Pit holes, by the roadside, with a Zeal of Capela!!

A bright child with shinning eyes,

All over the ,monsoon with glowing dyes!!

A glimpse of Globe in that little mind was full of naughtiness!!

A wish to playfully enjoy her childhood was affirming her doughtiness!!

"Ahh, a life is trapped over the Pit Hole", She exclaimed!!

"I should help it to come out of the blockhole ", She exclaimed!

She goes nearby the Life and saw a small puppy was in a terrific condition,

With her hands, in the swamp of water, she helped the puppy to come out!!

The puppy was shivering continuously,

His condition was deteriorating rapidly!!

With Only few limited resources,

She wrapped the puppy in her sweater!!

And started running towards her house,

Holding the puppy in her lap,

Slowly, the puppy's condition started to improve!!

This small act of wisdom had made the little girl a True douse!!

20. A Hiding Palette

She rushed into her room and covered the puppy with a blanket,

She put on the Room Heater and ran into the Kitchen for some Hot Milk,

Meanwhile , the puppy opened his eyes a bit and took out his head from the placket,

With Silent Little footsteps , she brought the milk, though by the act of bilk!!

She started feeding the puppy little by little,

And the puppy begin to acknowledge small,

Though he tried , but from his mouth ,the milk spilled!!

The situation was quite a brawl!!

"Dear, when did you come back from school?

And why you did not change your uniform yet, of school?"

" Mother, I came from school some time back!

And busy in rehabilitating a puppy with brack!!"

The mother surprisingly asked, "Which puppy you are talking about my Dear?"

" We do not have a puppy in our house mere!!"

In response to this she begin to narrate the entire story,

And her mother seems to be quite happy to be a part of this Tory!!

21. Growing Together Onto the Ages

Puppy and the girl were growing together, With each passing Day,

With laugh and laughter every day was passing with immense gay!!!!

Everyday, the puppy used to eagerly wait for the girl to arrive from school,

Once she arrives, they used to cheerfully eat and play together, rolling memories into spool!!

Little did they cater to others, more involved into each other's,

Carefully being pride of each other, more safe they would feel when around each other!!

A little did they bother about their surroundings,

More would they complete their groundings!!

Munching onto many feasts which mother used to prepare

They always used to overwhelm hope onto despair!!

Crunching the Life's twists and turns,

They were sailing onto a creamy churn!!

Often the growing age's complexity ,could not make their wishes down!!

They were self believers, one with the action and other with the words,

And they used to easily express their Frown!!!!

And they continue to make beautiful chirred!!

22. A Sudden Plight

Nurturing those days of Innocence and Childhood,

They were stepping onto the age of Adulthood,

One with her words and the other with his actions, they are now Fully grown Girl and a Dog!!

Proved to be the two most strongest pillars of the entire House like a Hood!!

"Quick, Quick, please allow us to move faster, we need to save their Father!!"

On a cloudy evening, a sudden burst of calamity, banged their Peace of Haven!!

The mother was driving and rushing to the hospital, along with the girl and the Puppy, accompanying her husband,

All were tensed and stressed, they could not measure the End!!"

" Doctor, this is an emergency, please save him!!"

Everything around was so dull and dim!!

"Mam, please be patient and allow us sometime to identify the cause "

All of a sudden, the lives of these people came to a Pause.

The mother and the child were onto Tears rigorously,

Looking into this situation, the Dog brought a bottle of water consoling them lovingly!!

"This is a critical condition, Please Pray to God", the Doctor voiced out !!

And hence, everything was Greyed Out!!!!

23. A Miracle

Hearing all this, the mother had become mum and fainted,

She was rushed to a hospital bed with a set of dip,

Though the Girl was brave enough to handle the situation

Still, she had completely emerged herself in a state of confusion and sadness,

And eventually she had lost the Grip!!

The Dog was terribly in pain , but he was wise Enough

To trigger a Spiritual Act which can make these Hard Times Light from Tough!!

He Hold the Girl's hand Tightly, and took her to a Prayer Room!!

And they both started chanting to Almighty, so that the medicines act like a Boon!!

"Your patient is recovering, This is a Miracle " the Doctor screamed with a Good Hope!!

Their eyes startled and glittered all around,

Everything seems to be lightened all surround,

They ran towards the Cabin to see their Father within the Clinical Bounds!!

"Mom, please open your eyes and be alright, Father is ok now,

Me and Our Dog, we both prayed together to God and slimed our Head to Bow!!

We kneeled down to the Most Superior, to save our Father,

I was dumbstruck even, to think anything when you and Father were not together,

Nevertheless, our Dog had held my hands Firmly and took me to the Prayer Room,

He had showed his real Smartness and Care towards us,

He is our Real Saviour!!"

24. A Peaceful Goodbye

Few Days later, everything around was regaining its good shape,

And all the things were falling onto its places!!

Father was released from the Clinic and,

He was recovering with a smile in his face that was overpowering scrape!!

And once again there was a moon of Contentment,

And Once again there was a misty noon of commencement

All the Demons and Evil were vanishing gradually,

And the Peace was restoring Slowly!!

"Mom, This morning Our Dog has not waken up yet,

He has not been a prompt responsive since few days!!

Let us take him to the Doctor!"

"Sure, let us take him immediately!! "

The Doctor replied" He will not be alive for many days from now!!

A small mass of nerves are bulging out like a prow!!

He is in a deep pain which cannot express., but only with his actions,

Please take good care of him in his last few days!!"

Listening to Doctor, their world has almost stopped,

Greeting a Goodbye, will be very tough!!

Those few days they tried to the Zenith, to keep him up and Running,

He also reciprocated the same and accepted the weaning!!

Finally he left them with some best memories thus far,

Though he was gone, but his Wisdom, Loyalty and Care were their integral part,

The family misses him everyday,

His absence is felt by the Family in every activities and in every now and then,

However, they have accepted that he is no more with them.

Moral :

Each and every moment of our Life, whether beautiful or ugly, is short lived. Whatever the moment is, give your cent percent, be honest in all the perspective of Life, be it on Prayers, or in any other context and wait for the magic that will happen.

The Most Unseen !!!

Lying on the Bed, often she ponders,

Glancing the Night Sky, More frequent she wonders!!

Gulping through her eyes,

Perhaps the Shine, her curiosity seize!!

Gone are those days of Purity!

When often the time passed enjoying the serenity!!

Thumbing the impression of Sanity,

Now often we feel the Urge for Clarity!!

A Lure of Vacuum enlightens the Sky,

A dormant sadness over the Horizon , Shy!!

Though the magnificent Glow is shinning up the Blue,

Although we tend to listen to the Dazzling Around than
True!!

An Infused Shine

Every Dark Forest says it's Own Stories,

Caring For the People and Providing the Love Breweries!!!!

Beholding it's Strong Roots, Standing Tall and Calm,

When Wind Blows, They Murmur their Own Music,
though they stay Mum!!!!!

As the Sun Rises, Thy Glow Slits their Own Growth,

Though They Hesitate, Still They Allow the Sunshine to
Invade Their Domain!!!!

It Hits, Agonizes and Releases it's Toxicity,

Though Harsh, But It Becomes Their Brutal Reality!!!!

The Pain of Leveraging Their Freedom to the Sunshine,

Tears Them Down As Early Morning Mists, but they still
Align!!

Nevertheless, They Are More Silent, And They Are
Enough Patient,

Eventually the Day Passes By and A Brighter Day Shines
Up!!

The Mists help them to Spread their Glow Even Larger,

And Here They Become More Resilient Than Ever!!

With the wonderful shine each day now,

They have become the most beautiful Trees to Bow!!

Emancipation

25. The Discipline Within

Up Holding to the Best Behaviour,

Grooming to the Strict Discipline!!

He was a true example of paviour,

He was bold enough ,to act, what he used to imagine!!

Starting his Routine with the crack of Dawn,

Gaining Momentum with the moment of sworn!!

Training his mind and Body to Achieve Big,

He used to pat his back on small victories with an Act of Jig!!

Glorifying his hard Work to a Long run Ambition,

He was protruding his Future as a Beautiful Carnation,

Often he used to admire his Foundation,

All the people around, used to respect his Determination.

26. A Stand For Self

He was full of clarity towards his way out, to his hereafter

He was bold and certain for his Desirable Future!!

Focusing on his Examinations and, concentrating on his Outcomes,

He used to get inspired with this little Win Crumbs!!

Looking at his Aspiration,

Admiring the way he used to Obey to his Yearning Protocols

His Guardians were always very supportive of his Intention

Though Failures were an integral part of his journey,

They used to nurture him and his goals, whenever they used to Fall!!

An unforeseen case had thumped his and his family's affairs

His father lost his job to the unprecedented errs!!

All his trainings were suddenly paused due to non payment of Fees,

Hence a moment within, his hopes of acquiring his Goal was Ceased!!!!

• 83 •

He never used to loose his focus even in difficult Times,

Although he could not go for the Training,

He used to rehearse what it was trained thus far in these difficult times!!

Eventually, he initiated a Coaching Centre for the Children around for his Fees and Future Campaigning !!!!

27. Harsh Struggles

This was never going to be an easy journey for him and his Family,

It was full of Sorrow and Profanity,

Riveting on one self and other Trainees was very Tough,

Convincing the People around to send their Kids for training was a Ambiguous Stuff!!

Hence a month or so, when his Trainees started gaining a Push,

And his pupils gaining disciple with this Routine, in a whoosh!!

People all around, started accepting him with a Progressing Heart!!

He was gaining Familiarity amongst many Villages surround, because of His Game and Art!

All of his fights and struggles were never supposed to go in vain,

Though he could not get a chance to continue his trainings,

He was rendering fame!!

Some Time hence, he had become the Most Self taught Cricket Vein!!

28. A New Beginning

Many Tournaments and competitions were held for his Trainees,

And in every Event, they proved to be the Best!!

With every Match his Trainees used to play,

And they secure the highest Rank with Ease!!

All over the Villages and Towns, his fame was shaped as Wonder,

And people from different cities and town want to admit their children in his Training Centre!!

From a small piece of open land where he used to practice and preach,

He runs several Coaching Institutions in Town and Cities for aspirants to Teach!!!!

His own Coaching Centre where he was not allowed to continue his training,

Seems to invite him as a guest Guide!!

Once when he was fighting his battles all alone,

Despite his Guardians, now are with him as a Fraternity and Backbone!!

29. A Leap To Triumph

He used to ponder often, "Whether I was supposed to become a Coach?

I wanted to become a Cricketer, and make my country broach!!

Do I was not competent enough to continue?

Or I was not competent enough to Miscue?

I tried but I failed, not because of my Hard work!!

The inadequacy of Money in my family made me to Quit

I was determined enough to go through the Hard Phases,

I was convinced enough to turn my desire into Blazes!!

Am I a lifetime Failure?

No, I quit from my individual Desire!!

At the same Time, I had hold Many Aspirants like me to Grow,

Nevertheless, I will continue to serve upon my mission,

And I should be able to keep the zest alive on me,

I should be able to make hundreds of Faces To Glow ,with their Victory Flow!!"

And He continues on his Harsh Path of Life,

He continues to keep his Zeal Alive!!

We hope to see him to go further and Beyond!!

He was born to become an Inspirer and hence his Success Stories Flaunt!!!!

Moral:

Never Loose Hope on Yourself and Always Focus on your Goals. Some way or the other your Good Intention and Ambition will be fulfilled, if you are persistent in your Efforts.

Amidst Nature

He comes from the world of glory,

He reigns to the world of Beauty.

He thrives to score the wisdom' storey,

Though, He emerges as a sustain fluky.

On a mission to captivate a green kingdom,

That occupies an itinerary more random.

On a trial to achieve the Nature's crown,

He dare her abilities to go beyond.

He wants to travel all around the World ,and make his own Way of Living

He wants to exemplify, to let people discover the way of sieving.

He used to believe that, staying positive is a kind of
Leisure,

And Leisure is the one that determines our Future.

Here He goes with his own sense of freedom,

And Builds his own kind of Liberty.

Here he goes with his own way of structuring a
Queendom,

And the Nature makes his Assays Worthy.

Where Gravity Hails

Upside Down, A Tilted Crown,

Amidst Sea, The Sun Drowns!!!!

Grasses behold the roots of the Ground,

Which gets the Soil and Earth Bound!!!

In a world full of mayhem,

Hunting begins for a soothing Bethlehem!!!

Where the peace turmoil and the surfaces disarray,

I time travel and the happiness replay!!!

Growing through the Life's Thick and Thin,

Glowing to a Daydream that Flickers In!!!!

I urge the way out of my Imagination,

Aspiring to accept the path of Ambition!!!!

A Starry Night

All over the sky, there are tiny little stars,

All can feel the brightness, though we are resting so Far!!

We try to share this grief seldom,

Often the sky feels a comfort place for our boredom!!!!

An illuminous spread that gets in through the Window,

Touches the Walls of the Room and the Toe!!

The majestic Glory of the Sight, keeps us awake and
Wonder,

The Charm of the Scenery, fills our Heart with Beauty
and Curiosity Sunder!!!!

The Roars of the Thundering up above the Sky,

Makes our ears feel like a melodious Lullaby!!

The Glow of that Pole Star thus high,

Makes our eyes a glittering Pie!!

We wish for once, we could have got the chance to get closer to them,

To feel theirs Enchanting Aura,

And To Nourish their Dreamy Tiara!!